Original title:
Branches of Belief

Copyright © 2025 Creative Arts Management OÜ
All rights reserved.

Author: Nora Sinclair
ISBN HARDBACK: 978-1-80567-188-6
ISBN PAPERBACK: 978-1-80567-487-0

Rising from the Ashes

In the land of the quirky, belief can wear hats,
A talking potato claims he knows where it's at.
He dances on table, with a toothpick for grace,
While squirrels debate how to win the next race.

Here comes the cat dressed in a tuxedo so fine,
He says, "Join my club, we'll sip on some brine!"
The dog starts to howl, with a bass in his bark,
As fish in the tank form a band in the dark.

There's a ladybug preaching on the garden path,
Spreading the gospel of carrot cake math.
While ants in their suits hold a meeting, you see,
Discussing the merits of dancing for tea.

And as winter approaches, the cactus turns blue,
Proclaiming, "I'm ready for a snowball or two!"
With laughter exploding, the leaves start to sway,
In this world of oddity, we dance and we play.

Echoes of Assurance

In a land of cheerful chat,
Eager minds discuss the bat.
"Is it true?" asks a pesky flea,
"That faith can fly higher than me?"

Squirrels debate in lively tones,
While raccoons munch on ancient bones.
"If you believe in spaghetti sauce,
You'll find it leads you to the boss!"

Badgers nod with a giggly grin,
As hedgehogs spill the beans within.
"To find a path that's truly bright,
Just dance with moonbeams every night!"

Plenty of laughter fills the air,
As critters swap tales with flair.
"If your sandwich trusts the jam,
All our worries will go 'wham!'"

Threads of Devotion

Knitting circles spin and twine,
Making scarves that look divine.
"If you loop your yarn with a wish,
You'll catch the stars in a bright dish!"

Cats jump in, they just can't resist,
Helping out with a funny twist.
"With faith you might just find a mouse,
Or maybe even a tiny house!"

With every stitch, laughter glows,
As dogs remind us of their woes.
"When faith wears pants that really fit,
You'll dance through puddles, never quit!"

Friends gather round with crazy schemes,
In threads of joy, they weave their dreams.
"Let's make s'mores without the fire,
A challenge that we all admire!"

The Canopy of Understanding

Under a tree that laughs and creaks,
Curious critters gather at the peaks.
"Do leaves know secrets, oh so grand?"
"Of course! But they don't take a stand!"

A parrot squawks out ancient lore,
While squirrels argue—"No! It's a chore!"
"Is chat with the sky a grand affair?"
"Only if you don't lose your hair!"

Bugs offer wisdom, tiny and bright,
"If you hug a cloud, it feels just right!"
All disagreements end in cheer,
As everyone joins in a fun-filled leer.

Faith is like gelato in a cone,
Full of flavors you've never known.
"If it melts, just lick with glee,
Understanding's sweet as can be!"

Vines of Tradition

In the garden where grasses dance,
Old tales twist and make a prance.
"What's tradition?" a flower asks,
"It's the way we wear our quirky masks!"

Laughter twirls as daisies sway,
While pumpkins joke about the day.
"If your roots are strong and spry,
You might just learn to touch the sky!"

Frogs jump in with oddball schemes,
"Tradition's found in wacky dreams!"
"Do frogs and tigers share a tale?"
"Only if tigers don't try to bail!"

Vines do climb and twist around,
In shades of laughter, they're tightly bound.
"So grab a giggle, don't let it go,
In every twist, let joy always show!"

The Contours of the Cosmos

In the sky, a donut floats,
With sprinkles that make wise old goats.
Stars whisper tales, oh so absurd,
About jellybeans that sing when stirred.

Aliens dance in polka dots bright,
Claiming the moon is their disco night.
And when they beam down to Earth,
They ask for fries, what a quirky birth!

Sunbeams toast marshmallows with glee,
While comets race for a T-shirt spree.
Every planet has its own hobby,
Neptune crochets, oh isn't that snobby?

Laughter echoes in the cosmic sea,
Where gravity's just a silly spree.
So if you doubt this celestial flight,
Join a planet's party every night!

Fables of the Heart

Once a squirrel lost his sense of cheer,
He claimed love was like nuts, never near.
A wise old crow cawed in delight,
"Just share your stash, and don't take flight!"

Two skunks argued over the best scent,
While raccoons plotted their little event.
A party where all could feel romance,
With trash-can treats, they'd surely dance!

A turtle wore a heart on his shell,
Said, "Getting love is like climbing a well!"
But with every slow step, he found his way,
To a cute little rabbit who joined him to play.

So in the forest, love found its groove,
With mismatches and giggles, they all move.
In the fables of hearts, let laughter shine,
For love's just a party, with snacks divine!

The Quietude of Conviction

A snail with a cape said, "I believe!"
In a world where everyone takes their leave.
"I'll win the race with style so grand,"
He plans to glide, not a care at hand.

A cat thinks naps hold the secret key,
To wisdom found under the oak tree.
"Every snooze is like a deep debate,
And my dreams only help me relate!"

Amidst the flowers, a frog plays the lute,
Singing of truths, while chasing his suit.
"I'll jump for joy in my slimy attire,
Conviction is boring, but tunes can inspire!"

Owls hoot nonsense while wisdom goes wild,
Who knew that silence made the heart child?
In the quietude where the curious meet,
Laughter is the answer, oh isn't that neat?

The Geography of Belief

There's a castle made of chocolate bars,
Where gummy bears meet under the stars.
The sweet tooth kingdom won't take a stance,
On whether to eat or join in a dance.

Penguins debate in the land of ice,
How sliding on bellies sure feels nice.
While polar bears ponder the warm sun's glare,
"Is this a sauna, or just fresh air?"

Cacti strategize in the desert's heat,
To convince a tumbleweed to dance on its feet.
"It's all about posture!" they announce loud,
While wind carries giggles over the crowd.

Maps of knowledge drawn with crayon flair,
With every twist beyond despair.
In this geography where humor stays,
Life is a journey, in zany ways!

Coins of Confidence

In a pocket of dreams, I found a dime,
Tossed it in wishes, but missed every time.
I chuckled at fate with a wink and a grin,
Who knew such small currency could make me feel thin?

With each shiny coin, I bought silly thoughts,
Like dancing with squirrels and wearing green spots.
I bartered my doubts for a bright, crazy hat,
Turns out confidence lives in the craziest spat!

I flipped one for luck, it landed on tails,
Spoke to a pigeon, regaled him with tales.
We laughed at convention, we joined in a spree,
A quirky parade where the world looked like me!

So here's to the coins, that jingle and jive,
They jumpstart the heart, they keep dreams alive.
With pockets of laughter and wishes galore,
Each coin's just a ticket to open the door!

Waters of Wisdom

I dipped my toes in a puddle of thought,
Found ripples of wisdom in moments I sought.
With rubber duck courage, I floated around,
In a sea of ideas, serenity found.

A fish with a top hat shared jokes from the deep,
Spouting puns and riddles while I couldn't sleep.
'If you swim with the flow, be sure to dive in,
The wisdom you catch may lead you to win!'

I splashed through the nonsense, soaked up the fun,
Understanding can't sink when your heart's on the run.
The currents of laughter can wash doubts away,
So bring on the waters, let giggles sway!

With every drop falling, I learned to unwind,
Embraced all the silliness life left behind.
So dive into the pool of the quirky and wise,
You'll float above troubles, beneath sunny skies!

The Clockwork of Ideals

Tick-tock went my dreams, caught rhythm and rhyme,
Wound up in banter, I lost track of time.
With gears set to chuckle, it clicked into play,
Cogs spinning brightly in a colorful way.

I tuned my ideas to a zany old song,
Found harmony in humor where the weird didn't belong.
The hands on the clock did a waltz on the wall,
While wisdom pirouetted, absurd and enthralled.

A pendulum swinging to laughs on the air,
Counting giggles galore, spun without a care.
Each second a tickle, each minute a grin,
A whimsical watch where the fun would begin.

So here's to the clockwork, all gears turning fast,
Where passions collide, and laughter is cast.
In the workshop of dreams, I'm crafting my scheme,
With humor as fuel, I'm chasing a dream!

Tapestries of the Unseen

In a loom full of laughter, I wove up a jest,
Stitching quirks together, it turned out the best.
Each thread held a giggle, a puff of delight,
Creating a fabric that's whimsical, light.

With colors so vibrant, and patterns so strange,
Every knot told a story, inviting a change.
I tangled in merriment, spun tales with a twist,
Crafting a tapestry, I simply can't resist.

The unseen can tickle, can twist in the air,
Like a cat wearing stripes, or a shoe in a chair.
The threads of connection, they bind us in cheer,
In woven discoveries, my heart finds its steer.

So let's dance on our looms, let's weave with our glee,
The unseen is playful, just wait and you'll see.
With laughter as fabric, and joy as the seam,
A tapestry grows, unfurling the dream!

The Spectrum of Faith

In the church of mismatched socks,
Preachers dance with silly clocks.
Their sermons fly like paper planes,
While doubts do summersaults in chains.

Holy water's just tap from the sink,
Miracles brewed in a cup of wink.
Faith is like a game of charades,
Where answers hide in silly tirades.

Angels sport a chilly grin,
As they slide down a rainbow thin.
The faithful stir their morning brew,
In mugs labeled 'Faith or No. 2?'

But laughter's the road we will take,
With joy found spilling from every quake.
In this wacky world, we dare to play,
With hues of belief that brighten the day.

Landscapes of Certainty

In fields where dreams are planted high,
Cows question the clouds in the sky.
The sun plays hide and seek with the grass,
While squirrels debate on which nuts to amass.

Llama teachers hold classes each noon,
Teaching science with a fork and a spoon.
Confidence grows like wild weeds,
Chasing butterflies, planting seeds.

Mountains giggle at valleys below,
While rivers hurry to outflow and glow.
Certainty hiccups with laughter and glee,
In this wild landscape of you and me.

When the map is a doodle, we don't even care,
We travel on foot, with the wind in our hair.
With every stumble, we find a new cheer,
In this quirky land where all thoughts persevere.

Reflections in the Mirror

Oh mirror, mirror, who's the fairest of all?
A puppet or a jester, standing tall?
With silly hats and mismatched shoes,
It whispers wisdom in giggles and blues.

The truth spins like a wacky top,
As the face inside begins to bop.
Some days a hero, others a goat,
All on a float, in a wobbly boat.

The reflections giggle, and so do we,
In the carnival of who we can be.
Painting our stories with glee and flair,
While hidden questions dance in the air.

So let's toast to the zany parade,
With mirrors that reflect how we've played.
In the end, being ridiculous feels right,
For what's life without laughter in sight?

Seeds of Hope

In gardens where chuckles sprout like flowers,
Hope tickles roots with giggling powers.
The soil hums a harmonized tune,
As sprouts dance under the nodding moon.

Each little seed tells jokes to the rain,
While worms audition for a stand-up fame.
They waddle and wiggle, with glee so bright,
In this soil where all things unite.

A sunflower grins, with its head held high,
Saying, 'With humor, we can reach the sky!'
Twirling and swirling in every breeze,
Sharing sunshine and quirky stories with ease.

So let's plant our laughter, and let it grow,
With every chortle, our garden will glow.
In the world of whimsy, we find our groove,
As seeds of hope dance, and the heart starts to move.

The Heart's Compass

In a world of maps and signs,
There's a path where humor shines.
Follow laughter, not just trend,
With each giggle, hearts can mend.

Lost my way, but oh, who cares?
With jokes to share, I climb the stairs.
Turn left at silly, right at play,
My compass spins, I'll find my way!

Footprints in the Sand

On a beach where seagulls tease,
Tiny footprints, oh what a breeze!
Each step giggles, makes a sound,
In the sand, joy can be found.

Waves crash, but I just grin,
Splashing water, let the fun begin!
Every footprint tells a tale,
With laughter echoed—never pale.

The Embers of Aspiration

In the fire where dreams ignite,
S'mores and jokes make spirits light.
Marshmallows toast, then drop and fall,
Yet every slip brings laughter's call.

Chasing sparks, with friends so dear,
Roasting hopes, they disappear!
But we cheer and stoke anew,
Aspiration, through laughter, grew!

The Arc of Trust

Trust is like a trampoline,
Bounce too high, you lose the scene!
With friends beside, we laugh and leap,
Catching moments, joy we keep.

If you fall, don't take it hard,
Just roll a bit, then play your card.
In this dance, we find our groove,
With every twist, we find our move!

The Frontier of Belief

In a land where folks debate,
A chicken crossed, oh what a fate.
Was it to find some truth, they say,
Or just to scurry out of the way?

One claims a sign from above,
Another insists it's just a shove.
When cats can talk, the world grows bright,
But logic shrinks, oh what a sight!

A tinfoil hat for the wise old coot,
Claiming the earth is shaped like a fruit.
While squirrels steal the acorn stash,
They laugh at the humans' silly clash.

So hold your beliefs with a wink,
Just don't forget to stop and think.
When faith gets tangled in a jest,
Just choose the fun—it's truly the best!

The Kaleidoscope of Feeling

In a world that's full of cheer,
Colors swirl with each loud cheer.
Red for love, and green for the humor,
What's blue again? Maybe just a rumor?

A man with tangerine shoes,
Claims he knows the cosmic blues.
While dancing cats pour tea on time,
Jumping in rhythm—oh, what a rhyme!

On Mondays, we wear silly hats,
And whisper secrets to the bats.
The moon's a disco ball at night,
Twinkling down in playful light.

So grab your heart and twist it right,
With every spin, take off in flight.
For feeling's just a crazy game,
And who's to win? Oh, who's to blame?

Foundations of Purpose

A builder with a wobbly floor,
Says, 'Every brick must have rapport!'
He lays them down with utmost care,
While squirrels dance up in the air.

The architect can't find his plan,
He thinks it's lost, oh what a span!
With each misstep, the laughter grows,
As coworkers spill their coffee flows.

The purpose is a lofty aim,
To build a tower just for fame.
But what's the use if joy's not there?
A giggle shared can bless the air.

So stack your dreams like silly blocks,
And hope they don't resemble socks.
For purpose thrives where humor dwells,
In laughter's bell, all magic swells!

The Harmony of Belief

A band of dreams plays out of tune,
With jumbled thoughts, they start at noon.
The trumpet prances, the drums just roll,
Each note a tale with comedic soul.

The singer thinks she's lost her keys,
In a shoe! Oh, what a tease!
While dancing ducks join in the song,
They croak and quack and sing along.

The harmony is not so neat,
But who needs rhythm when it's sweet?
With each discord, the laughter grows,
In chaos, kindness often flows.

So join the band, don't miss a beat,
Embrace the quirks, oh feel the heat!
For joy's the thread that weaves the tune,
Where laughter blooms beneath the moon!

The Dance of Understanding

In the realm of thoughts we play,
With ideas dancing in a fray.
A jig of logic, a waltz of chat,
Turning serious minds to flat-out pat!

Twisting like pretzels, minds in a spin,
Understanding comes from where you've been.
A leap of faith, a sidestep or two,
Finding common ground, who knew?

Bouncing on truths, like they're a trampoline,
A springy approach to the unseen.
In laughter we find our way to the core,
What once was a struggle, now we explore!

So tango with theories, cha-cha with glee,
In the dance of minds, come twirl with me!
For knowledge is better when shared in jest,
Join the party, it's simply the best!

Temples of Thought

In the temples of our minds we tread,
With quirks and quirks, we're never misled.
Cobbled beliefs and loose-fitting views,
Turns out they're just funny little shoes!

Shouting secrets at the outer walls,
Echoes of laughter, a chorus that calls.
Turn down the seriousness, let's add a quirk,
In these hallowed halls, we're just at work!

With pillars of wisdom that wobble and shake,
We construct our faith, oh what a mistake!
Minds do a limbo, bending so low,
Ah, the beliefs that dance like a show!

So let us gaze up at the skies above,
Finding humor in thoughts we think we love.
In the temples of thought, we jest and we play,
Turning the serious into a funny ballet!

The Paradox of Serenity

In quiet moments, we seek to decree,
A paradox of calm that's really quite spree.
With zen-like poses, we try not to laugh,
As our thoughts race by like a speedy giraffe!

Serenity's a puzzle, wrapped up in glee,
Where peace takes a backseat to the comedy,
We sip our tea, and trip on our mats,
Finding calm amidst giggles and chitchat!

As silence shouts louder than the loudest song,
We find our stillness and it feels so wrong.
Chasing tranquility, we stumble and slip,
Beneath the surface, the bubbles still rip!

So let's dance in the storm, let our spirits ignite,
In the paradox where laughter feels right.
We're searching for peace, but we'll take the jests,
Finding serenity's punchlines are the very best!

The Altar of Intent

On the altar of ideas, we place our best hopes,
With sticky notes swirling like colorful scopes.
Setting our aims with a wink and a nod,
What's serious to one is a chuckle to God!

With candles that flicker and slight bit of sass,
We offer our plans and watch them amass.
Intentions like balloons, float high in the air,
But watch out for the breeze, they could go anywhere!

We gather our thoughts, like fireflies bright,
Hoping to catch them before they take flight.
In the chaos of life, we seek to align,
But we embrace the goofy, it's simply divine!

So bow at the altar, make laughter your lead,
With humor as fuel, it's a delightful creed.
For intent is a journey, not just ends or starts,
As we navigate this maze, let's pick up some hearts!

The Forest of Faith

In a forest of giggles, we dance like trees,
Twirling our worries, ignoring the bees.
Each leaf whispers secrets, a playful delight,
As squirrels debate if the sun sets at night.

The branches are ticklish, they laugh in the breeze,
Convinced that they're wise, but they barely can sneeze.
They gather in circles, reciting their charms,
While the owls roll their eyes, watching from the farms.

With each rustle of foliage, wild tales unfurl,
Of fairies in pajamas and a pogo-stick swirl.
The roots gossip softly, their laughter is deep,
As the laughter of faith fills the forest we keep.

So come join the fun in this leafy retreat,
Where belief is a joke, and good vibes are sweet!

Petals of Persuasion

In a garden of giggles, persuasion takes root,
With petals of charm and a playful dispute.
The daisies are daring, their colors so bright,
While roses make puns, just to lighten the night.

Sunflowers are strutting, all tall and so proud,
While tulips are gossiping, forming a crowd.
They argue in whispers, then burst into song,
Claiming the gardener's right all along.

With every sweet blossom, a story unfolds,
Of bees with big dreams and butterflies bold.
They sway to the rhythm of laughter and cheer,
And convince every cloud that sunshine is near.

Petals of persuasion, with humor they bloom,
Creating a garden that banishes gloom!

Leaves of Loyalty

In a tree of camaraderie, leaves cling tight,
Bonded by laughter, they shine in the light.
They share silly stories, and wriggle in glee,
As the wind twirls their secrets, just like a spree.

Oak leaves are old souls, with wisdom to spend,
While young maple sprouts giggle, 'Who needs to pretend?'
With ribbons of sunlight, and giggles galore,
Every loyal friend knows there's always room for more.

In the brush of their laughter, they promise to stay,
Through winter's cold whispers, come what may.
They'll rustle together in a colorful dance,
Proving loyalty's found in the silliest chance.

So sway along branches, let joy be your guide,
In this lively ensemble, there's nothing to hide!

Trunks of Truth

The trunks stand there sturdy, with tales to confess,
With knots like old timers, who jest without stress.
They'll chuckle through seasons, with humor and grace,
In the shade of their stories, all wishes find space.

Bark wraps the wisdom, with laughs from the past,
They'll joke about summers that never clashed.
Each ring tells a snapshot, a punchline in time,
With jests about squirrels that climb for the prime.

As the sun peeks through leaves, it highlights the fun,
While truth takes a bow, saying, 'Life's never done!'
There's humor in honesty, even when tried,
For in the heart of the trunks, all the laughter resides.

So gather 'round nature, where giggles run free,
In the stronghold of truth, come and join in the spree!

Blossoms of Certitude

A cat thinks it's a tiger, bold,
It struts around, its ego uncontrolled.
The pigeons watch with heads held high,
'Who needs a loom when you can fly?'

A squirrel claims that acorns are gold,
While gripping his stash, so daring and bold.
He stocks up for winter like a king in his lair,
But all he has is old nuts and air.

The duck quacks loudly, claims he's a sage,
Philosophizing 'gainst the bird-cage rage.
But who will heed an aquatic bard,
When wisdom floats in a pond, so marred?

In this grove of thought, so jolly and bright,
Each creature debates through day and night.
With laughs and giggles, they sway, they prance,
In folly's embrace, there's always a chance.

Reflections of Reverence

The wise old owl, he wears glasses thick,
He reads the night sky and thinks it's a trick.
'If stars are just pinpricks in heaven's dome,
Then who needs a map? Just follow your gnome!'

The hedgehog believes he's a knight in disguise,
With spines for armor and a heroic rise.
He charges at shadows, ready to fight,
But often he just gets scared of the night.

A sheep in a sweater thinks he's so grand,
'There's wisdom in wool, you won't understand!'
With every baa, he lays down his plan,
While the grass simply giggles, 'You're still a lamb.'

In this realm of laughter, respect wears a grin,
As creatures debate where reverence begins.
With quirks and quirps, they flit to and fro,
In this funny faith, we all share the show.

Silhouettes of Sincerity

A fox with a top hat, so dapper and neat,
Claims all he needs is his dancing feet.
'With a little finesse, a dash of panache,
I'll win the whole forest with one single flash!'

The raccoon, our bandit, insists he's a star,
'Who needs a sofa? Just look at my jar!'
With trinkets that twinkle, he spruces his lair,
But really, it's just junk he found here and there.

The parrot goes viral, his jokes take flight,
'Polly wants acorns, and wisdom so bright!'
Yet every time he drops a new pun,
The squirrels just roll and say, 'Here we run.'

In this theatre of shades, where sincerity reigns,
Every critter brings laughter, breaking old chains.
With gestures so grand, and banter so sweet,
We cherish the joy in our wild little suite.

The Orchard of Opinions

In trees made of chatter, fruit hangs all around,
Each topic a morsel, in laughter we're drowned.
The apple says 'I'm the best in the lot!'
While oranges yell, 'Nah, we're hotter, a lot!'

The cherry claims flavor, the berry weighs in,
With juicy debates, let the tasting begin!
While the bananas all giggle with peels in the air,
'What's fruit without fun? We aim to declare!'

Plums ponder colors, while grapefruits discuss,
Who's tart and who's sweet, in this juicy fuss.
But in the end, as laughter ascends,
All fruit holds a place, no matter its bends.

In this orchard of thoughts, so lively and bright,
Each bite brings a chuckle, a burst of delight.
With every opinion, so wacky and free,
We savor the sweetness of our fruity decree.

Constellations of Conscience

In the sky of thought, oh what a sight,
Stars are dancing, some left and some right.
Like a toe-tapping fool at a wedding spree,
One twirls on truth, another on glee.

A comet zips by, what a dazzling show,
While asteroids blend with opinions that flow.
Galaxies whisper their secrets so grand,
But who really listens? Well, no one had planned!

Black holes of doubt try to suck us in tight,
While planets of logic spin day into night.
Aliens giggle from their distant spheres,
At our misadventures mixed with our fears.

So let's toast to the stars, all quirky and bright,
In this cosmic circus, it's all quite a fright.
Confetti of questions, each answer wears shoes,
At this party of ponder, we win—who can lose?

Crossroads of Thought

At intersections where ideas collide,
Traffic signs point, but none can decide.
One way says "logic," while the other says "fun,"
We're stuck in a roundabout, where thoughts weigh a ton.

A squirrel in a tie gives a side-eye of doubt,
Suggesting that maybe we should just shout!
"To the left!" says the rabbit, "no, to the right!"
But the hedgehog just snores, "It's all a delight!"

GPS of wisdom, recalculating fast,
Takes us through corridors of "what if" and "past."
We're bumper-to-bumper in this mental parade,
With joy and confusion, a grand escapade.

So let's park our doubts by the hot dog stand,
Where thoughts blend like ketchup in silly demand.
With laughter as fuel, and a smile in the air,
We'll drive through the chaos without any care!

Hues of Harmony

In a palette of life, colors swirl and play,
Red argues with green, "Let's brighten the day!"
Blue adds a splash, "No crying, just cheer!"
While yellow is grinning, "We're all friends here!"

The brush strokes of laughter paint shadows of doubt,
As purple gets dizzy from all the clout.
"A splash of confusion!" cries pink in delight,
While orange just giggles at this colorful sight.

The canvas expands with each silly glimmer,
As hues shake their hands and their voices grow dimmer.
"What shade am I feeling?" says turquoise in glee,
But emerald whispers, "Just be, let it be."

So we throw our brushes in the air with a cheer,
United in chaos, creativity near.
With each silly stroke, our uniqueness ignites,
In this gallery of giggles, we're all taking flights!

The Seed of Surrender

Once a tiny seed took a trip underground,
Feeling quite lost in the darkness it found.
"Should I sprout up now? Or wait for a sign?"
As worms giggled, "Just chill, you're doing just fine!"

"Why rush?" said the acorn, "Just wiggle a bit,
Take your sweet time! This all is quite lit!"
Roots brushed together, they formed a big cheer,
As the seed let go of its worry and fear.

The ground softly chuckled, "Embrace your own pace,
Life's not a race, it's a magical place!"
So the seed stretched its leaves, with a grin wide and bright,
Finding joy in the wait, oh what a delight!

Now a splendid flower, it sways in the breeze,
With petals like giggles, it aims to please.
It learned that to bloom, sometimes you must rest,
And the art of surrender? Oh, it's simply the best!

The Alchemy of Belief

In a cauldron of thoughts, I brew,
Silly notions tossed in, just a few.
Mixing laughter with a wink,
Who knew faith could be so pink?

Potions spill on the floor,
Why do I believe? Ask the door!
It creaks with wisdom, it seems,
To dream big, just follow your dreams.

With wands made of spaghetti, we strive,
Giggling as our quirks come alive.
A sprinkle of humor, a dash of cheer,
Turns heavy hearts into a hearty sneer.

So let's toast to the absurd, my friend,
In this wild game, there's no end.
With chuckles and jests, we'll find our way,
In this alchemy, we laugh every day.

Veins of Reverence

In the roots of thought, we play,
Silly beliefs lead us astray.
With jester hats and playful cheers,
We shake our heads at all our fears.

We dance with shadows, twirl with glee,
Who knew reverence could be so free?
A rubber chicken in hand, we prance,
Faith becomes a joyful dance.

Knock-knock jokes with a twist of fate,
Open the door to a humor state.
For every solemn thought we find,
A goofy twist comes up behind.

With chuckles echoing through our veins,
We turn our woes into playful chains.
In this realm where laughter reigns,
Reverence blooms, even in silly stains.

The Fabric of Faith

Stitching moments with a thread so bright,
Tangled tales fill the fabric tight.
Quilting dreams with snippets bold,
Faith wears colors that never get old.

With patches of humor, we mend the seams,
Each laugh a stitch, weaving our dreams.
A button pops, and oh what fun,
In this tapestry, we're never done.

Frayed edges tell tales of delight,
Whimsical threads dance in the light.
We twirl our beliefs, a fabric show,
Sewing joy wherever we go.

So wear your faith with a wink and a smile,
In this fabric of fun, let's stay awhile.
For every quirk and thread so slight,
Creates a picture of pure delight.

Bridges to the Sacred

Building bridges with gummy bears,
Connecting hearts with silly cares.
Every step bounces with a joke,
On this path, no need to poke.

Wobbly beams, but look at us go,
Faith in laughter makes us glow.
Each giggle echoes over the span,
Can't take it seriously, who could plan?

With marshmallow ropes, we pull along,
Singing silly tunes, our raucous song.
Every leap we take, a laugh is found,
On this bridge, humor knows no bounds.

So let's skip along our playful way,
Finding joy in each and every day.
With every chuckle, a step we take,
These bridges to the sacred are ours to make.

Threads of Destiny

In the web of fate, I tripped,
My pants split wide, oh what a crypt!
Spinning tales of life and glee,
While cats debate who's the best me!

A knit one, purl two, but I lost count,
Now it's a scarf for my pet—what a mount!
My destiny's tangled, never quite neat,
But hey, who knew chaos could be this sweet!

Jesters laugh while I weave my way,
Through yarns of yarns, come join my play!
In every knot, a joke awaits,
My destiny forks, but I'll take my dates!

So let's toast to fate, in this funny flair,
With threads that laugh and tickle the air!
Each loop a giggle, every stitch a cheer,
Life's silly fabric is what we hold dear!

Portals of Perception

Through a door, I flipped upside down,
On the ceiling, I wore a crown!
Perception's a trickster, nothing so clear,
Yet my cat thinks I'm the top engineer!

I peered through the glass, what did I see?
A chicken in pajamas, dancing with glee!
Reality's funny, like socks gone rogue,
Twisting and turning like some bizarre vogue.

What's real and what's not? I can't tell you quite,
This portal's a circus, a merry delight!
A fish on a bike, a cow in the sky,
In this odd dimension, we just laugh and sigh!

So swing by my portal, let's roll on the floor,
Chasing our senses, who needs to keep score?
In this world of wonders, we're all a bit mad,
But the best kind of crazy is the fun that we had!

The Nexus of Dreams

At the nexus of dreams, I took a ride,
On a unicorn that has something to hide!
He wore a tutu and bright red shoes,
In this dreamland, you just can't lose!

The clouds were fluffy cupcakes, oh what a sight,
With frosting rainbows twinkling at night!
I shared a joke with a drowsy bear,
While squirrels played poker without a care.

Up there, my worries danced with the stars,
Whizzing past planets, imagining Mars!
But then I tripped and fell down a slide,
Straight into a pool of jelly with pride!

The dreams collide in a laughable mess,
In this nexus of nonsense, nothing's less!
So bring me your laughter, your wacky delight,
We'll dream up a storm every whimsical night!

Galaxies of Faith

In galaxies far, where giggles abound,
I saw a duck with a rubbery sound!
Floating in space with a comical grace,
Quacking out love from the Milky Way's face.

A telescope showed me aliens in hats,
Who debated the merits of friendly cats!
In cosmic cafes, they sip bubble tea,
Sharing their dreams and glee like a spree.

Stars twinkled brightly, like sequins so grand,
While shooting stars made a rock band!
Each note a wish, a silly refrain,
Echoing laughter through the cosmic domain.

So let's dance in these galaxies spun,
Where faith is funny, and laughter is fun!
In the universe's heart, we'll find our place,
In this wacky adventure, let's embrace the grace!

Clusters of Contemplation

In a tree of thought, thoughts take flight,
Squirrels debate day and night.
One thinks he's wise, a sage so grand,
While the other munches nuts, quite unplanned.

Branches sway with laughter, quite absurd,
Twigs competing for the best word.
Leaves chuckle as they tickle the breeze,
Jokes about acorns, oh what a tease!

Bark whispers secrets, crude and funny,
Every knot a tale, oh so punny.
Roots below shuffle, trying to hear,
While branches giggle, without any fear.

So sit under this scholar tree,
Where wisdom's a joke, you'll agree!
Contemplation clusters, in haphazard glee,
Join us for laughs, it's free, just be!

Canopies of Contusion

Under this canopy, ideas collide,
A jumbled mess, no need to hide.
One leaf says 'yes', the other 'nay',
While birds chirp gossip, all day.

Branches stretch out, in awkward poses,
Sharing their thoughts, how silly that grows!
A twig tried to fly, but oh, what a flop,
The whole forest giggled, so they just can't stop!

Roots tangled up, playing peek-a-boo,
Who's got the wisest thought, who knew?
Vines swing in laughter, wrapped up tight,
In this chaotic scene, pure delight!

Canopies of confusion, oh, what a sight,
Where the sun shines down, and everything's bright.
Join the wild party, don't be shy,
Under this bough, let's just fly high!

Whispers of Faith

In the quiet rustle, secrets are shared,
A nutty philosopher, who's slightly impaired.
His thoughts sprout wings, and take to the air,
As the leaves start to giggle, 'Oh, do we care?'

Pinecones confide in the gentle breeze,
What is truth? Who knows? Let's just tease!
A squirrel claims he saw the great bird,
While the robins just chirp, 'That's utterly absurd!'

Even the shadows play hide and seek,
Rustling with laughter, without a peak.
Faith here is fluid, like sap in the spring,
Dancing through doubts, oh what joy it brings!

So listen close, to the whispers so light,
Where even the moon chuckles at night.
With humor at heart, and lightness of soul,
We stand together, as one, whole!

Threads in the Tapestry

Threads of belief weave in and out,
Stitching together laughter and doubt.
One's a bright yellow, another's a blue,
Together they giggle, what a fine crew!

Each stitch a story, each knot a joke,
Unraveling wisdom, oh what a poke!
A tangled affair, with colors so bold,
Old grandmas chuckle, with stories retold.

Though some may fray, and others may thrum,
In this wild fabric, we dance and hum.
A tapestry of thoughts, woven with mirth,
In our quirky world, we find our worth!

So gather 'round, let's thread the fun,
In this lively quilt, we're never done.
Laughs intertwined, with each tiny seam,
In this crazy fabric, we dream our dream!

Conduits of Truth

In a world of quirky claims,
Truth often wears odd games.
One says cats can really fly,
While another swears pigs can cry.

With each wild tale that we spin,
Believers gather, let the fun begin.
A chicken crossed, for luck and glee,
But who's in charge? Not you or me!

Hats made of foil, they protect,
From aliens and their suspect tech.
You'd think the sun would start to hide,
When laughter joins the crazy ride!

So grasp your faith, but don't take flight,
For every jest hides some delight.
In this circus of quirks we see,
There's humor woven joyfully!

Shades of Assurance

With shades so dark, the doubts we block,
Wearing our faith like a trendy clock.
Unicorns prance just out of sight,
A dance of laughter, day and night.

Some shout their truth with great bravado,
Selling beliefs like a used avacado.
We chuckle soft at every twist,
And question when we feel we've missed!

In a soup of certainties boiled bright,
Pasta of nonsense slips out at night.
Spoons of wisdom stir up the fun,
While doubts get tossed 'til the morning sun.

So wear your shades, and wear them proud,
In the loudest echoes, don't be cowed.
For in this garden of wild jest,
The humor blooms, we love it best!

The Echo Chamber

In this echo chamber, who speaks true?
One voice yells nonsense, just for you.
With every bounce, a giggle grows,
As outlandish tales steal the show!

A rumor spins like a topsy top,
Gathering steam, and it won't stop.
"Did you hear about the dancing bee?"
"Oh yes, and it buzzes, just like me!"

In circles tight, we spin and twirl,
Crafting debates that cause hearts to swirl.
While sages laugh at the riotous sound,
They nod along, all merry and round!

So let's raise a toast to all the fun,
To echoing laughter and puns undone.
In this charming loop, we find delight—
Turn up the volume! It feels just right!

Lanterns in the Dark

In darkened woods where shadows sway,
Lanterns flicker, keep fears at bay.
One sparks a tale of grand delight,
A ghost with shoes that shine so bright!

We walk the paths of whispers low,
Stumbling on truths we barely know.
With giggles echoing 'neath the moon,
Conspiracies dance to a silly tune!

Guide us now with lanterns bright,
For faith is fun, a playful sight.
The more we share, the more we jest,
In realms of thought, we find the best!

So raise your lights, let laughter soar,
In the night's embrace, let's all explore.
For in this journey, joy's the key,
With silly tales, we all agree!

Pathways of Perspective

In a land where socks still mismatch,
Cats debate the size of their patch.
Dogs claim they know what's best for the sun,
But squirrels insist they're just having fun.

On Tuesday, the moon decided to dance,
While chairs held a council on how to prance.
The fridge hummed gospel to the pots and pans,
And the cat just laughed at all of their plans.

A toaster thought it could sing like a star,
But only popped toast, not going too far.
Coffee cups shimmied in sync with the brew,
While the spoon said, "Hey, can I join in too?"

With giggles aplenty at the garden's edge,
Flowers wore sunglasses, oh, what a pledge!
The world spins around with jokes on the line,
While ants hold a party and all feel just fine.

Inklings of Hope

A penguin in shades stuck his head in the snow,
Said, "Ice on my toes! That's a fabulous show!"
The robot next to him beeped out a grin,
While flamingos debated just how to begin.

An octopus juggling had everyone stumped,
"Is it more like art, or are we just chumped?"
The jellyfish floated with utmost delight,
"Float like a leaf, dance like a kite!"

Then came a llama, with a hat oh-so-fine,
Declared it was time for a fishy divine.
They all made a pact, swirling tales in the air,
That hope sprouted brightly, as light as a prayer.

A squirrel told secrets to a wise old tree,
Who nodded along, saying, "Just let it be."
The world spun in laughter, as hearts learned to cope,
With inklings of joy and the magic of hope.

Mirrored Certainties

A mirror once whispered to a sly silver spoon,
"That tea with the honey? It's gone way too soon!"
The table chimed in, "Let's not fuss or fight,
We're having a ball; everything feels just right!"

Reflections were sorting their shoes with a cheer,
While a cactus complained that his friends weren't near.
"What's certain in life? Is it more than a jest?"
A gopher piped up, "Just be sure to invest!"

Then came the debate of a vase and a sprout,
Who said that their friendship was filled with doubt.
But a curious fly buzzed and shared with a grin,
"Each petal and leaf holds the magic within!"

So under the sun, with shadows to think,
They stirred in a circle and raised up a drink.
Mirrors may waver, but laughter stays bright,
In the world of certainties, everything's light!

Fronds of Fellowship

In the heart of the park where the laughter is loud,
Fronds of green met pals, a most whimsical crowd.
A parrot gave speeches on how to be swank,
While turtles debated who'd fill up the tank.

A beaver brought snacks made of twigs and of leaves,
While hedgies and rabbits spun fun with their weaves.
The flowers all giggled, as petals would sway,
"Let's dance like it's spring, just for today!"

"Who says trees can't jiggle?" an oak let out cheer,
"Let's celebrate life with a spin and a beer!"
And the crickets played tunes that would brighten the skies,
While the sun snickered softly, sharing warm sighs.

Through lessons of kindness and fun-filled embrace,
Fellowship glimmered with laughter's warm grace.
So gather your crew, call the wild and the keen,
In fronds of connection, we're all evergreen!

Fragments of Faith

In a garden of odd dreams,
Grew a plant of quirky schemes.
Each bloom whispered silly lore,
About a squirrel who wanted more.

The sun wore shades, the rain did dance,
A faith that's more a merry prance.
"Let's believe in cookies," they said,
As crumbs of wisdom danced in bread.

Some argued for the power of fries,
While others claimed the truth in pies.
Banana peels and a dancing cat,
Who knew belief could taste like that?

The flowers giggled, petals bright,
While critters held their dizzy fight.
In the garden, joy was always near,
With every silly thought brought cheer.

The Cultivation of Hope

We planted seeds of silly dreams,
In pots of laughter, bursting seams.
Expecting beans to sprout up high,
But grew a squash that sang and fried.

With watering cans all filled with cheer,
We nurtured hopes both bright and queer.
A radish wished to wear a crown,
While pumpkins rolled their way to town.

The sun advised them to be bold,
Said, "Don't wait for hands to hold!"
So lettuce wore a dapper tie,
A dandelion flew up to the sky.

With every chuckle, weeds became friends,
In the garden where bright joy transcends.
Mirthful moments were sprinkled on top,
In this patch where caring won't stop.

Networks of Perception

In the web of quirky thought,
Nonsense tangled, laughter caught.
A spider spun her tales with glee,
"Can you believe in ants on a spree?"

A thought networked like wifi rats,
Trading memes for funky hats.
The more they shared, the more they knew,
That ticklish truths could sprout and grew.

Connecting giggles with a leap,
Thoughts of chickens who'd never sleep.
A quirk here, a pun over there,
One snail belief raced beyond compare.

In this maze of silly schemes,
Ideas danced in crazy dreams.
The network buzzed, a joyful scale,
As they plotted pranks without fail.

Seasons of Reflection

In winter's chill, a snowman dreamed,
Of summers hot with ice cream streamed.
"Oh, let's believe in melted cheer,"
He chuckled loud for all to hear.

Spring arrived with giggles bright,
As bunnies launched a feather fight.
Colors sprouted, funny and bold,
While flowers whispered secrets told.

Summer sizzled, all sun and fun,
A watermelon race had just begun.
They played charades with sunburnt clues,
And danced around in silly shoes.

Autumn brought a quirky flair,
With pumpkins dressed in vibrant wear.
Each season laughed as time flew by,
In reflections of joy that made us sigh.

Roots that Nourish

In the garden of thoughts, we all plant,
Some say it's a fig, while others chant,
One grows sweet dreams, another grows fears,
Watered with laughter, and sometimes with tears.

Mushrooms believe they're the life of the show,
While daisies just giggle, not wanting to grow,
A sunflower whispers, 'Look at my height!'
But roots in the dirt just shake their heads tight.

The carrots wear glasses, all proper and neat,
While tomatoes just lounge, like they're at the beach,
"Life's a big salad," they all seem to know,
Toss in some dressing, and watch it all go!

In this patchwork of soil, confusion thrives best,
Each plant thinks it's wise, but who's passed the test?
Raise your glass, garden friends, all rooted in jest,
Let's laugh as we grow, it's truly a quest!

The Symphony of Belief

In a world where beliefs play a grand tune,
You'll find the flutist wearing a spoon,
The drummer, a cabbage, keeps perfect time,
While a cat with a trumpet sings nursery rhyme.

The violins wail like an old, creaky door,
All the notes in the air make folks beg for more,
A tuba plays doubling as grandpa's old chair,
While everyone dances, with no hint of care.

A cloud in the back drops a rumbling beat,
Rainfall percussion, it can't be beat!
One tree waves its branches, conducting the show,
While bushes all bop to the rhythm we know.

Walking on stage, the squirrels take a bow,
In this symphony wild, they are all the 'how.'
With laughter and joy, the music will soar,
Join the funny parade, it's belief's folklore!

Mosaics of the Heart

Pieces of feelings like chips on a board,
Funny shapes and colors we can't afford,
A heart made of laughter, with giggles and cheer,
Missing some tiles, it's all crystal clear.

A patch of wild dreams sits right next to doubt,
They bicker and quarrel, both wanting the clout,
While joy wears a cape, flying high in the sky,
And sorrow in flannel just drifts on by.

The laughter, a puzzle, flips upside down,
Fitting in wrong, it just makes us frown,
Yet when we unite, like pieces that fit,
A masterpiece forms, oh isn't it lit?

In this gallery made of what we perceive,
Each tile tells a story, in what we believe,
So let's all get chippy, with humor as art,
Creating our mosaic, a fun-loving heart!

The Balance of Convictions

On a tightrope of thoughts, we wobble and sway,
Each step is a chuckle that leads us astray,
With beliefs in one hand, and humor in the other,
We juggle our truths like a carefree brother.

While wisdom wears slippers and dances with time,
Ignorance twirls, thinking it's sublime,
The scales tip and totter, what balances best?
A punchline or two, and we all get some rest!

In the circus of principles, the lions all roar,
While clowns in the background just beg for encore,
Each act is a lesson on how not to fall,
With laughter as safety net, we stand tall!

Let's toast to our whims, and the oddness of fate,
For balancing beliefs can truly be great,
With giggles as guideposts, we'll dance through the day,
In this funny arena, come join in the play!

The Meadow of Meaning

In a field where thoughts run wild,
A cow once pondered, strangely mild.
"Is the grass really greener?"
She chewed her cud, the ultimate patina.

A sheep jumped in with a wooly shout,
"I think it's just envy, there's no doubt!"
The cow rolled her eyes, quite unabashed,
As the sun set down, their worries dashed.

A pig strolled by, with mud on his face,
"Joy is splashing in a warm embrace!"
"But what if it rains?" said the cautious cow,
"Then we'll just dance and laugh—oh wow!"

So round they went, in a mud-stained spree,
Each thought was a giggle, oh so carefree.
In this meadow where meanings collide,
They found pure laughter, their ultimate guide.

Stems of Sentiment

In a garden where feelings bloom bright,
A rose told a daffodil, "You're quite the sight!"
"Pretty, but prickly," the daffodil grinned,
"But can you dance? Or are you just pinned?"

The tulips giggled, swaying in glee,
"Let's start a conga, come dance with me!"
The thorns rolled their eyes, with forceful jest,
"Watch the petals, they're under duress!"

"Why can't we bicker with charm and with grace?"
The daisies chimed in, each with a face.
"Let's cultivate joy, not just greet with sighs,
For life's a bouquet, let's color the skies!"

And so they twirled in a whimsical show,
Each stem self-quoted, "I told you so!"
In the garden of sentiment, such cheer so divine,
They laughed through the sunlight, feeling just fine.

Waves of Wisdom

On the shore where seagulls like to preen,
Sat a wise old crab with a thought quite keen.
"Life's like the tide, it ebbs and it flows,
But why wear your shell, everyone knows?"

The clams clapped shells, with eager delight,
"Your wisdom is deep, oh crustacean knight!"
"But wisdom is funny," the crab wriggled so,
"It gets really heavy when you've nowhere to go!"

A fish flopped near, with a bubble of cheer,
"I swim with my thoughts, without any fear!
And on days I'm lost, I simply just float,
For even fish dream of a colorful boat!"

So they laughed at the waves, while flinging their tales,
Crafting a life without worries or gales.
In the ocean of wisdom, absurdity sparkled,
As they danced with the currents and all giggled,
unbarreled.

The Grove of Ideals

In a grove where ideas love to parade,
Stood a tree with a sign, "No plans to evade!"
A squirrel laughed out, "Now that's quite absurd,
What's a thought without some, like, action inferred?"

A wise old owl perched high on a limb,
"Let's ponder these thoughts while we're singing a hymn.

For ideals are fickle, they dance and they dive,
But wouldn't it be great, if they come alive?"

A rabbit hopped in, with carrots to spare,
"Why bother with thinking? Just munch and don't care!"
The owl gave a hoot, "But think of the stew!
A thought stirred with carrots can spice up the crew!"

And so in this grove of idyllic delight,
Thoughts mixed with laughter, from morning till night.
Each whimsy took flight, as they learned to embrace,
The fun in the ideals, each quirky face.

Enigmas of the Faithful

In a church sat a cat with a hat,
He claimed he could speak with the big man in white.
The congregation laughed, patting their knees,
While the cat twirled around on the pulpit, delight.

A dog jumped in, barking loud with a grin,
Said, "Your prayers are as silly as my wobbly spin!"
The cat tipped his hat, with a wink in his eye,
"At least I'm the one with the divine fashion win!"

They formed quite the crew, with a pig and a goose,
Discussing the cosmos, yet counting on juice.
Their worship involved jumping, a dance and a roll,
To see who could best praise, and still keep control.

In this town of delight that was full of pure jest,
Belief soared high on a cow's back, no less.
They sang through the streets, neighbors joined the fun,
Laughing as faith turned a hoedown to run!

Cadence of the Mind

A scholar declared with a flick of his pen,
"The universe spins like an old vinyl then!"
As he scribbled and scrawled with a bit of a flair,
His thoughts took off like a wild, comical air.

With equations that danced, he puzzled the crowd,
Chasing down truths that were mighty and loud.
"I'll solve life's great questions, won't need to play chess,

Just give me some snacks and a top hat, no less!"

Philosophers argued, ate fries by the score,
While pondering if they had too many before.
Each thought flew like popcorn from kernels not popped,
Their theories, like bubbles, just fizzled and flopped.

But amidst all the chaos, they stumbled on grace,
As laughter filled rooms with a warm, smiling face.
They found truth in their folly, wisdom in jest,
In the cadence of minds, they were truly blessed!

Whispers Through Time

Two ghosts in a library, floating about,
Spoke softly of secrets, of fables and doubt.
"I once saw a zombie who danced with delight,
He groaned out a concert on a dark moonlit night."

The other one chuckled, a banshee named Claire,
"That zombie's got moves, but no soul to spare!"
They giggled away at the thought of his sway,
As each shelf of old books seemed eager to play.

In between the tall tales and echoes so bright,
They wove a strange tapestry of joy and of fright.
"Belief is a dance, though it varies in style,
Sometimes we just shimmy, sometimes we walk a mile."

As whispers of wisdom flowed slow through the air,
All the tales and the giggles became somewhat rare.
Yet even in shadows, they found glimmers of light,
In the dance of the fables, belief shone so bright!

Vistas of Inspiration

A painter once stood at the edge of a cliff,
With colors that sparkled, a very bold gift.
He swirled blues and reds, with a wink of his eye,
A masterpiece forming as clouds floated by.

An artist nearby, with a spoon and some peas,
Said, "Why not use snacks? They're a canvas, if you please!"
They cooked up a storm, with a smile and a cheer,
As visions became dishes, oh what a career!

They painted the town with their chatter and flair,
With laughter and snacks, spreading joy everywhere.
Each brushstroke a giggle, each meal a delight,
Inspiration flowed freely, transforming the night.

With canvases bright and a meal to divine,
Their beliefs were a feast, oh what a fine line!
For art can be edible, and fun can be wise,
In the vistas of life, joy finds endless skies!

Leaves of Understanding

In the yard, I saw them dance,
Little leaves, teasing in chance.
They whisper secrets all day long,
In a language that feels so wrong.

One slipped and fell, caught on my hat,
'Look at me!' it shouted with a spat.
The others laughed, a leafy crew,
All in jest for me to view.

As I pondered, a twig did say,
'Understanding's just a leafy play!'
They spun around, so merry and bright,
Turning my confusion into light.

And when autumn came, I sighed,
Their silly dance, I could abide.
For in the rustle, I found my glee,
Leaves of understanding set me free.

Constellations of Trust

Under the stars, I saw them shine,
Twinkling beings, all perfectly aligned.
They made a pact, oh what a fuss,
Each one promises, in the cosmic bus.

A star snickered, 'Let's play a game!'
'Trust me!' it winked, without any shame.
'I'll shine for you, the brightest I can!'
But fell right down, what a cosmic plan!

Another declared, 'I'll guide you home!'
But zigzagged wildly across the dome.
'Oh dear stars, can't you stay true?'
They giggled, 'Trust is hard for us too!'

Yet in their chaos, I found a light,
A silly twinkle in the night.
Constellations of trust, so full of jest,
In their confusion, they shine the best.

Tides of Worship

The ocean rolled, a funny swell,
Its waves sang tales, in a watery spell.
Each tide would rise, then fall, it seems,
In a dance of worship, like crazy dreams.

'Oh mighty moon,' the sea did cry,
'Come closer, let's give it a try!'
But the moon giggled, 'I'm way up here,
You splash and crash, I'll just disappear!'

The fish all joined with a splashy glee,
Singing hymns in a fishy spree.
'Worship with us, it's quite the swim,
Let's dive deep and sing a hymn!'

Yet every wave that danced around,
Stretched and laughed without a sound.
Tides of worship, full of play,
In the ocean's jest, I found my way.

Petals of Perspective

In the garden, petals twirled so free,
Colorful laughter, they beckoned to me.
'Come join our party, we'll show you the way,
To see the world in a bright array!'

One flower said, 'I'm red, can't you see?
But check out my friend, she's yellow with glee!'
Another piped up, 'I'm just a wee bud,
But I've got the wisdom of a great flood!'

The daisies chortled, a merry bunch,
Mixing colors like a funky punch.
'Perspective is key, try on a new hue,
You might just find a fresher view!'

So as I wandered through this bloom,
Each petal shared its own little room.
Petals of perspective danced in my head,
In their laughter, old fears fled.

Cracks in the Facade

A sage once said, with a wink and a grin,
"I know everything, just let me begin!"
But when asked about socks, confessions were bare,
He muttered and stuttered, "I can't take that dare!"

The world's full of quirks, yet he knows all the rules,
Dancing around logic like johnny with jewels.
His crystal ball's cracked, it shows blurry dreams,
But who needs the truth when you've got all these memes?

With wisdom that wobbles, like jelly on toast,
He'll tell you what's fair, as long as you boast.
Certainty's funny, it slips through the cracks,
While doubt roams freely, with snacks in its packs!

So here's to those sages, with tales often spun,
Who laugh at the questions, yet still seek the fun!
In the cosmos of chaos, they giggle and peep,
Finding joy in the process, a mystery to keep!

The Oracles of Today

In a world full of filters and polished poise,
The oracles speak, oh what a strange noise!
With hashtags of wisdom, they spin their tall tales,
While skeptics roll eyes, hoarding popcorn in pails.

"Like, follow for truth!" they declare with a smile,
As likes become lore, turning thoughts into style.
They squint into screens, their crystal replaced,
And predict tomorrow with a well-fitted face.

But what if the wisdom they share is a bluff?
Like asking a cat, "Hey, are you tough?"
Their insights can giggle, yet dazzle with doubt,
In this circus of truths, we all dance about.

So trust in the antics and humorous spins,
The oracles tease us, but oh how it wins!
With laughter as guidance, let's all take a ride,
In the dance of the foolish, where wisdom can hide!

The Weave of Wisdom

In a loom of confusion, threads dance all around,
Wisdom is woven, but often unbound.
With colors of laughter, and stitches of glee,
We question the fabric, yet feel so free.

A tapestry rich, with patches askew,
Each pattern a lesson, with nonsense in view.
From the great and the wise to the silly and small,
Each loop seems to giggle, just waiting to fall.

The wise may have secrets, but humor's the thread,
Weaving joy in the chaos, while chasing our dread.
With logic and laughter, we mix and we blend,
Creating a quilt that we'll share with a friend.

So let's stitch some fun in our quest to believe,
In a world that's a riddle, we just need to weave!
The fabric of life may fray at the seams,
But with smiles and mischief, we'll follow our dreams!

Horizons of Certainty

Out on the shoreline, we gaze at the tide,
Searching for answers, with seashells as guides.
The waves splash around, like jokes that we hear,
While seagulls debate the taste of our beer.

With horizons of certainty stretching afar,
Where questions and answers are never on par.
The sun has a wink, and the clouds start to bow,
As we ponder what matters, in the here and the now.

So we chuckle and ponder, with waves in our hair,
Embracing the doubts that float through the air.
For certainty's mirage, a shimmering game,
Is best served with humor, not fear or shame.

So let's relish the mystery, embrace the unknown,
With laughter as our compass, we'll find our way home.
For in our wild journey, with friends by our side,
We'll navigate life with a fun-loving guide!

Shadows of Conviction

In the garden of thoughts, funny ideas sprout,
The tomatoes wear hats, and the radishes pout.
Mice hold a conference, debating all day,
While cats in the corners just sleep on their prey.

Pumpkins claim they're wise, with laughter in tow,
Chasing their shadows, putting on quite a show.
A scarecrow recites his philosophy's tune,
As the crows start to clap, howling out 'What a boon!'

Sing, sing the anthem, of giggles and quirks,
For every odd thought is a puzzle that works.
Silly, absurd, but with meaning so deep,
In shadows we find what we laugh about, keep.

So gather your muses, don't hold back a grin,
In the wacky world, let the fun times begin!
Each laughter a stitch in this fabric we weave,
Creating connections, in jest we believe.

Whispered Faiths

Under the quilt of stars, we share tales at night,
Of socks that go missing, what a curious sight!
Do they dance in the moonlight or hide from the sun?
We ponder in whispers as laughter has begun.

Tea cups hold secrets, stirring up the brew,
While biscuits debate if they'll stick or fall through.
A wise old ladybug, gliding with grace,
Shares her views on the virtues of an empty space.

We're all just like ducks, with our quirks and our flaps,
Waddling through life with a few silly mishaps.
In whispers like these, the world shines so bright,
Finding joy in the jests through the chill of the night.

So let's crack some jokes, let the joy and fun flow,
In the chorus of chaos, we continue to grow.
Embracing the laughter, with hearts feeling light,
In whispered beliefs that make everything right.

Roots of Reverence

Deep down in the earth where the humor is lush,
Rabbits debate about who moves with more hush.
Their vows of allegiance in giggles they share,
While the squirrels just take nuts, with hardly a care.

The flowers all chime in, tickled by the breeze,
Conspiring to dance, bringing laughter with ease.
'Let's throw a party!' the daisies declare,
With confetti from petals, they float in the air.

The worms hold their meetings, plotting a play,
While the ants march around, in a curious ballet.
Nature's amusing gallery, living with pride,
In the roots of our laughter, where secrets reside.

So cheer for the moments that tickle your soul,
In this wacky wonder, each giggle's a goal.
From depths of the earth, let our joy rise above,
Entwined in the quirkiness, let's laugh and love.

Tapestry of Trust

Each thread tells a story, woven with delight,
Of socks that have vanished, and dreams taking flight.
A carpet of chaos, where giggles collide,
In the tapestry's dance, whimsical and wide.

Bees buzz their prayers, in harmonies sweet,
While butterflies flutter, tapping their feet.
The owls share their wisdom, with winks and a hoot,
As the frogs croak their vows, wearing shoes that are cute.

Through the stitches of laughter, we connect every day,
Finding joy in the jests, in our own playful way.
A tapestry vibrant, strong yet so light,
We embrace every stitch, turning wrongs into right.

So dance to the rhythm, let the colors unite,
In the humor of life, we find pure delight.
With threads spun in jest, let our stories unfold,
In the tapestry of trust, forever be bold.

The Core of Conviction

In the depths of my heart, a thought does spin,
Like a hamster on wheels, it can't let me win.
I dance with my doubts, they lead me astray,
Yet I laugh at my fears, they're just here to play.

My friends say I'm crazy, my logic quite bent,
I argue with shadows, but they never relent.
The truth is elusive, like socks in a wash,
Yet I'll prance in my chaos, oh what a frosh!

I preach to my cats, they nod, then they yawn,
One swipes at my nose like the dawn's early pawn.
I'm certain in jest, though my theories might wobble,
In my world of make-believe, I'm free to gobble!

So here in this circus, my mind likes to roam,
Each whimsy a canvas, each giggle a tome.
I'll stumble and fumble, but here's what I know,
Life's funny parade is the best way to grow!

Oaths in the Silence

In a whisper I vow, with my pizza in hand,
To spread love and joy, like jelly on sand.
The world might seem serious, but hear my decree,
I'll take my oaths lightly, with laughter and glee.

I swear to the cows that stare from the field,
To share my ice cream, my secrets unsealed.
In the quietest moments, my promises bloom,
Like a flower made out of an old vacuum!

When raindrops are falling, I pledge on my shoes,
To dance in the puddles, embrace all the blues.
I swear I'll be silly, a clown of the day,
For the best oaths are funny, they lighten the fray.

So gather your friends, let's giggle and sway,
With oaths that are silly, let's brighten the gray.
In the silence of laughter, where fun intertwines,
We'll whisper our vows, as the comedy shines!

Canopies of Thought

Beneath a wide roof of my quirky ideas,
I juggle my worries, like a clown with no fears.
Thoughts dangle like piñatas, ready to burst,
In the garden of nonsense, my laughter is thirst.

I climb up the branches where musings reside,
With squirrels giving pointers, they're along for the ride.
The wind picks up whispers, tickles my ears,
As I ponder the meaning of cheese through the years.

I pull on a thought, and it wobbles a bit,
Like a friend's awkward dance or a cat with a split.
My canopy's crowded, but I love every shade,
In this forest of jests, my heart's never weighed.

So here's to the branches that sway in the breeze,
Where wisdom wears sneakers and giggles with ease.
Let's camp in this treetop, sip tea with delight,
In the canopies of thought, we'll dance every night!

Labyrinths of Ideals

In a maze made of whims, I wander my way,
With signs that say 'Giggle' and 'Dance in the Fray'.
My ideals twist and turn, like spaghetti unspooled,
Yet I laugh at the chaos, not one thought is schooled.

I chase after dreams, but they're sly little things,
They flit like wild butterflies, teasing with wings.
Each corner I turn, there's a riddle, a pun,
And I can't help but chuckle, oh this is such fun!

I chat with a wall that insists it's a door,
It's hard to be serious when laughter's in store.
I sketch out the pathways with crayons and flair,
In this labyrinth of laughter, I've got naught a care.

So come take my hand, let's get lost in delight,
With the silliness swirling, we'll dance through the night.
In the maze of our minds, let's forget all the fears,
In the labyrinths of whims, let's gather our cheers!

Verses in the Silence

In a forest of whispers, I heard a loud crow,
Telling secrets of trees, to us down below.
A squirrel in a suit, gave a speech on a toad,
While the mushrooms debated the rules of the road.

Beneath a tall oak, a wise owl doth dwell,
Prattling on nonsense, with stories to sell.
He says that the leaves, they giggle at night,
But the rabbits think he's a terrible sight.

Each branch spreads a tale, each twig sings a cheer,
While the bees make their honey in whispers we hear.
A party of gnomes has begun on the grass,
With dancing and laughter, oh, time flies so fast!

Yet when morning arrives, the secrets all fade,
And the laughter of night becomes quite overplayed.
So we'll wait for the dusk, while the critters align,
To hear all the stories, in moonlight divine.

The Orchard of Dreams

In a garden of giggles, where dreams come to play,
Lemon trees whisper of lemonade day.
Peaches wear hats, sporting stylish designs,
While the melons debate about their fruity lines.

A carrot in glasses, reciting some prose,
While radishes ponder who's wearing the clothes.
"I'm sweet!" yelled the corn, with a puffed-out chest,
But it's clear that the beets believe they are best.

The flowers all dance in a polka-dot style,
With the sunshine above, shining bright with a smile.
The breeze carries laughter, from daisies that bloom,
As tulips tell jokes about fish in a room.

So join this fine harvest, of humor and glee,
For in this orchard, we all twirl free.
With apples in capes and strawberries on stage,
The chuckles abound, throughout every age!

Mysteries of the Unknown

In the land of the lost socks, a rabbit once said,
"The purple one's hiding, but blue's in my bed!"
A cat wearing glasses draws diagrams, neat,
Mapping out pathways for shoes and for feet.

Baskets of puzzles, their contents unwind,
With questions like, "Where does the sunshine unwind?"
A turtle recites all the lore of the time,
While ants in a circle plan pranks in their prime.

An echo of giggles spills down every hall,
As whispers of secrets come out at the call.
Floating in bubbles, ideas take flight,
While fishes in bow ties discuss the night bright.

So ponder the quirks, of the odd and the strange,
Where mysteries gather, and nothing feels plain.
With each quirky thought, we embark on a chase,
In the kingdom of laughter, we'll find our own place.

The Essence of Insight

A snail on a quest, with a magnifying glass,
Declared, "I'll find wisdom! Just give me some grass!"
With a wink of a bug, and a nod from a worm,
Philosophy bloomed, like a flower to learn.

A frog with a mustache, exclaimed, "Why so blue?
The puddles hold answers! It's all up to you!"
While crickets compose, with their symphonic cheer,
Proclaiming, "Each croak is a thought to revere!"

With berries reflecting, both giggles and dreams,
The branches of laughter have delicate beams.
For wisdom is silly, when seen through a lens,
Of giggles and chuckles, and delightful old friends.

So dance in the light, with a tickle of thought,
For in every small moment, insight can be sought.
In a world full of whimsy, let your mind roam free,
To discover the essence of pure jubilee.

www.ingramcontent.com/pod-product-compliance
Lightning Source LLC
Chambersburg PA
CBHW072147200426
43209CB00051B/834